HISTORIANS OF REDUNDANT MOMENTS

A NOVEL IN POEMS

Nandini Dhar

Published by Agape Editions
http://agapeditions.com
Los Angeles, CA

Agape Editions is an imprint of Sundress Publications.

Copyright © 2016 by Nandini Dhar
All rights reserved

This title was selected by Vandana Khanna as recipient of the 2016 Numinous Orisons, Luminous Origin Literary Award for Poetry.

Cover image: Red Dress, White Dots
Artist: Guda Koster
Image is used here by kind permission of the artist.

Cover & interior design: Kristen Camille Ton

Editors: Fox Frazier-Foley & Jasmine An

Agape Editions titles are printed using Lightning Source and distributed by Ingram Content Group.

This title is also for purchase directly from the publisher.

Library of Congress
Cataloguing-in-Publication Data
Historians of Redundant Moments // Nandini Dhar
Library of Congress Control Number 2016953038
Dhar, Nandini
ISBN 978-1-939675-41-5

9 8 7 6 5 4 3 2 1

FIRST EDITION

CONTENTS

HISTORYING THIS SYLLABIC LANDSCAPE   1

WALL HISTORY   5

MAKE-DO MOTHER MYTH   23

THIS TOWN: A BROKEN GLASS BANGLE   37

SPECTER HISTORY   55

CAUSELESS CATASTROPHES   81

A BRIEF HISTORY OF CLAMOR   105

NOTES   109

ACKNOWLEDGMENTS   115

HISTORYING THIS SYLLABIC LANDSCAPE

A harmonium abandoned in the middle of an empty factory
        cafeteria: a doll hanging by its head from the clothesline
in the courtyard. Two cats on the ill-kept lawn, fighting
        while the crow builds a nest on the walls of the forsaken

wedding banquet-hall: this is the city the cartographer
        is after. Here, in this urban legend, the oldest daughter
does not stand out. The youngest does not have to hide
        a pencil-knife in the seams of her hitched-up skirt.

Here, beyond the shadows of the reading lamp, two
        rabbits yawn together, two owls attempt to break open
in unison the glass shields of a palm-sized replica:
        Lenin's mausoleum. Two banyan trees stand side by side,

branches entwined in a conspiracy to demolish
        everything that is brick or concrete. The house-snake
rattles its bones inside the overgrown nayantara
        bush—twice. And we sisters, in keeping pace

with the rule of two, learn to reject the other
        more prevalent regimen—the rule of one.

        Yet there is only one slashed face of Jamini Roy's mother, only

        one of her son's lotus-petal eyes washed away by the night rain. Only

my sister's coloring stains on the wall—what remains
        of the blemishes—after our uncle made her
scrub them out with her tongue. Hand-sewn curtains,
        a blouse without buttons, the unwashed dishes: a home

is a city. A city is a home. A five-paisa coin thrust
        between her slitted lips, blue-bead eyes deboned,
her plastic skin pockmarked with ink-stains. On the forehead
        an oversized bindi stolen from the aunt's dressing-table drawer:

the doll's head is an uncharted city. A house purged
of dolls overflows with cautionary tales, oft-repeated. Repaired
into proverbs: *early to bed early to rise, honesty is the best policy.*
Listed wounds, chanted in hushed undertones: blistered

remembrance. A grandmother wakes and finds several
little girls inside her sari pleats. A mother breaks a long word
right through the middle—*toitombur*—into two, hides
them inside pickle bottles, takes them out after three days

to name her twin daughters. Here, behind the pumpkin
vines, two little girls are folded over and over again.
Transformed. Mutated: two nesting dolls. Interrogations narrated
in intimately plotted details. A story of a young man's

shriek in every tip of leaf. *Drippings from a suspended burning
tire* on an eighteen year old's back: Naxalbari is not the name
of a village only. Scraps of history on the little girls' eyelids,
their boycut hair, scars on the chins and weeping lips. Memories

that love to poke. The tips of a wound, an incision
right on the skin. Here, under the shadows of the porch light,
a mother teaches her twin daughters to spell
their names: backwards. A novel way to count our elegies.

This is also how fingers are inserted inside little girl eyes—uninhibited,
open, craving newness. Insistent ghosts. The result is a luminescent
entanglement—a broken doll-head, two little girls vacillating
in their choices—tiger, or spider, or both. Stretch this thought

into a pajama-drawstring: these little girls cannot be kept
hidden in the shadows of a rat's tail. In the stillness
of the window panes, they find their secret atlases.
In the cracks of the mattresses, the broken pebbles

embellished into admonitions. Until this becomes a game—who can
locate the glint of the sickle in the tininess of the spoon.
Who can excavate in the pile of unwashed dishes
the grammar of the rally chants. And vice versa. Neither

of them thought to count the ghosts. Even as children
        they knew. They knew in every promise a woman creates
with her blood, there is a ghost. And another. And another.
        A failed insurrection and its broken archives—the pasts,

presents, and futures of half-loves. Half-convictions.
        The shame and embarrassment of half-beliefs. A cow licking
its dead calf. Two little girls crack open a doll's belly.
        Inside: nothing. On a stick, the doll's head: execution.

The plastic torso: useless, to be donated to the Chief Minister's
        Relief Fund. With their feet in bear-print socks still dangling
above the ground, the sisters learn: restraint is not the biggest asset
        for anyone dreaming to be the cartographer of homes,

neighborhoods, cities, stillborn histories. This is only an example
        of what some will call

                          ghost discipline

I
WALL HISTORY

THE WALLS OF THIS HOME

A faint attempt to trace my fingers along these walls; too many pasts to unembrace. Too many catastrophes breathing through each others' mouths, trying to erase the inevitable prequels and sequels. Yes, we have left behind our child-brides hanging from the barbs on the wires. In this house devoid of nooks and corridors, cellars and parlors, we live without ghosts save those we have orchestrated from the detritus of demolished museums, unfurled flags, abandoned notebooks and misguidances. This game of hide and seek we play is nothing but our children's way of gauging, mapping, discovering—the uncharted corners that are not nooks, not corridors, not cellars, not living-rooms. An impeccably drafted map of mole-droppings, crumpled paper-boats in the farthest corners, pencil stubs inside drawers, a pocket-sized diary under the stainless steel almirah: pages torn, save for one. In it, in littlest aunt's round hands—*For you, always, Amitesh*. These chronicles—tossed out, discarded—beheaded remnants of a home. Our secret reservoir of stories: unnarrated. A tap on the wall, the sound of Tombur's head bumping the bedpost: *a home is where the clutter is*. A home is where possibilities come to petrify under humdrum havoc. An erased atlas, this burden of a hundred and one life-times: the walls of this home must become nothing but repetitive continents.

ARCHIVING REDUNDANCE

Mother goes around the house boxing things.
The attic is cluttered with old junk that we

children are not allowed to touch—suitcases wrapped
in white sheets, each with a label. **1943. 1948. YEH**

AZADI JHUTA HAIN. UNDERGROUND.
NAXALBARI LAL SELAM. 1977. Mother moves

around the house on tiptoe, brooms and rags in hand,
picking up all things that can be corralled—old fish bones,

newspaper clippings, torn pages from moth-eaten
manifestoes, shredded slogans, seams from old poem-quilts.

Afternoons she spends sorting these out, categorizing
for imminent encasing. Everything thus filed

under the right name, Mother settles
for her sweaty afternoon nap—mouth open, snoring.

ARTIFACT CARTOGRAPHY

The skull of a little girl, a miniature dinghy on fire, a ceramic doll's
house with a broken chimney, the wooden frame of a stringless guitar,

an ocean-floor of dead rats. What else can the rigid ribs of the walls
fit inside? A labyrinth of half-notated songs—my mother's. The wreckage

of a novel which never could be written beyond the first three lines—my
uncle's. Alphabets from a forbidden romance, the white space

of curves filled up by notes scribbled in illegible calligraphy—my
aunt's. The overabundance of meanings that can be retrieved from the torn

pages of *Dakshindesh, Deshabrati*. Whatever was left after almost everything
was confiscated. A tap on the wall, on our fingertips the evidence—in

this community, everything and everyone is unformed, fractured,
interrupted. A scratch of our fingernails along the walls—inside

every fissure of a brick, broken bones. Every piece
of peeled paint, shredded owl skin. A push with your head, thwack, bump.

The simultaneous revelation. Face each other, hand in hand,
the first timid articulation: *this is not where we can lean.*

What is left is a mangled promise. A silenced
sun hangs over the neighborhood. Nazia Hassan blares

assurance from the next door uncle's stereo.
I repeat *disco, disco, disco.* Like a scratched record.

My sister always and already alert about words,
whose meanings she does not know, is reciting

nashelee hain raat, nashelee hain raat, nashelee hain raat.
Mother peels off her skin to make a rag—to dust the dining-table.

Home, Mother says, is the shadow of an over-active quill.
Home, we sisters suspect, is our mother's bone sculpted into walls.

NO HISTORY BOOKS WOULD GIVE US THESE STORIES

Tombur and I hover in the attic, crawling
in between the boxes. We would have loved

to peek in, breathe through the rustling stories.
Yes, there were trains without passengers. Yes,

there were nipple-tips without women. And,
we are gobbling up their rustling remains.

But that was a long time ago—a termite-eaten
photograph, a trivial anecdote

that refused to be translated into the language
of facts. We never learnt to cook

in our grandmother's skillets. For there
were none. No famines.

No food riots. No rallies. No clandestine
meetings. No slogans. No protests. No

chants. No Chairman no Mao. No no no.
Instead: a trunk full of yellow-haired dolls.

A ship with a hole near the bottom;
full of porcelain animal heads—deer, tigers,

lions, cows and goats. A plastic
peacock. Its sequined tail fans out

at the touch of a switch. A song inside
its belly. A national anthem—stuck

repeating over and over again the same
two lines in the middle. These rooms. These beds.

Creaking with tales—lingering between forgotten
and recited. We would have swooped down

on them—these annals. Except that our fingers
were caught unspooling the threads from our dolls'

wedding dresses. White. Red. Blue. Fake silk. We
would have swooped down on them—these annals.

Except for the locks that keep whatever is inside
forever beyond our touch.

We lift white covers, lean
on the rusted metal exteriors, run our fingers against

the edges of the locks, press our ears hard
to rust, to figure out

if the clocks inside tick
like the one on our living room wall.

UNSEEN HISTORY

The sole glass figurine of an elf in between
the china teacups, soup bowls, dinner plates. No one ever

used them. Reserved for an auspicious moment, one that never
arrives. Under the coat of dust—persistent, hungry and angry,

the elf reflects on the color and shape of deception, the vicissitudes
of captivity. We would not have thought of granting him life.
Would not have thought of putting him in the same single
row as our other toys—the bear with a scar-mark on its belly,

the rabbit with only one ear, the blond-haired doll with a broken
nose. But Tombur promises she can swear

in the name of our very own Ma Kali. That she has seen
the imp leap, dance, wince. In pain, under the determined
strokes of Mother's cleanliness. In the same way we
wince, shake and cringe under the pressure of love

from those very fingers. Mother,
grandmothers, aunts—who, in order to earn their own keep
continue to braid the ricefields of our hair
into well-ordered parlors, plantations, teagardens.

And I giggle at my sister's fluency in profanity.
Giggle with my fingers pinched on my lips. This coupling of a promise

and an expletive that my sister has been aiming for. I hurt
my lips, because that's the rule. That little girls

should be protected against the sounds of their own laughter.

REDUNDANT PALATE

In the house where we are growing up, children aren't allowed to leave any food uneaten on the plate. Once upon a time, our grandmother was made to forget the color of salt, and as a result, nothing we eat is ever sprinkled with it. We spit out her saltless curries as soon as they touch our tongues. Grandmother rides a korai around the house, the end of her sari tight around her waist, pushing us towards confusing countries called *chewing* and *swallowing*. We do not remember the smell of our grandmother's sweat. We do not remember looking for gaps in the landscape of her skin. What we do remember is our grandmother standing over us while we eat, a bamboo-pole in her hand: *Is the hole of your throat too small to swallow rice? Do you want me to poke it bigger?* We twins, six years old, know this is no idle threat. So we eat.

HOW WE HISTORIED THE ROOM

Pull your knees back against yourself—stop walking,
learn to crawl. Along the walls, the cracks
on the cement floors, dust specks in the corners

of these rooms where women come to turn
into alphabets on pages
and men deceive themselves into feeling safe.

On the kitchen table are teacups, stains
on the rims, rattling with the wreckage
of memory: food riots, rally chants, police-shootings.

We crouch. Perched low, we cast our eyes into corners
where adult eyes cannot go. A room redesigns a child.
Tombur's knees knock against a steel almirah, my elbow

against the corner of the dressing table—sharp,
like a knife. A blister, a cut. In this room, where mosquito
nets tangle with ceiling fans, where a dilapidated bureau

wraps itself in a heavily starched cotton sari and begins
to grow an inch every day, we children
are trying to find a corner to stand.

All this clutter, Tombur whispers. A scratch
of our fingernails on the steel almirah. Between
our hands and our mother's saris inside,

dark alleyways, where the air stinks
like an unwashed baby bottom. A clasp
of our hands on the lips of the knob: between our fingernails

and the napthelene balls, a room at the end
of the alleyway. The grease from the palm lines
seeping into the air, too many noses breathing.

A 40-watt bulb, shading light, fingers
busy tangling, untangling, weaving
sinews into threads. The irksome embrace

we offer to these old saris. Between our ribcage
and their folds, charred bodies—an air heavy
with vulture plumage, no one's fault in particular.

A slipped ladder, a bricklayer, aged 13, dead.
So trivial that he was ashamed to turn
himself into a ghost. Unrecorded factory fires,

unnamed appellations: this room
which is shrinking, shrinking like wool,
like cotton threads after a wash,

under the pressures of unghosted factory aftermaths.

GRANDMOTHER HISTORIES THE FISH FILLETS

Grandmother teaches us that the fish
fillets are lost atlases. The bones: rivers

and cities on maps. We pore over
the riddles of fish names: boitka, balichura,

bamush, barali, bata, bele, batasi. Unoccupying
them of bones. Till our fingertips bleed, eyes

swollen. As we unoccupy the seams of our
skirts of sheyalkanta after an evening of hide-and-seek.

These bones so deft in escaping metaphors
 barely visible between our fingernails.

We wonder, what Grandmother thinks of the boxes
Mother takes so much care to keep locked. But all

Grandmother cares about are rice and fish, fish
and rice. And chewing the fishbone into shards.

CARNIVORE

We both know, this room is a silence
that devours children. Takes apart
their hair, their skin, spits the bones

out into the yellow hollows of streetlamps.
And we promise to each other: we shall not be deceived
by its paper-thin walls, the crisp

new widowhood of its ceilings. If
there is anything that can be memorized
from living in this house, it is this: the past

resides even in things that are new,
store-bought, without a single blemish. A woman
kneels on the floor, scrubbing the dirt

in the cracks. With every brush
of her finger, the crack
gets bigger. The woman,

who happens to be our mother,
does not notice. She is as formless
as air. This steel almirah

is only a week old. We watch
it grow hands, pull the woman by her hair.
Like bitter gourds from the vines.

She vanishes inside its ribcage. She
is spat out later, in the afternoon—a perfect
chocolate cake, replete with icing and birthday wishes.

MOUTH HISTORY

Inside the attic, in the company of boxes and white sheets,
our mouths bleed Cadbury

to heal from the smell of the fish-rice.

Our locked jaws the stage for encounters,
 massacres. Good children chew their food well.

Teeth, after all, are hoes. To separate bones
from flesh. We draw fish shapes

on metal boxes with spit, our mouths
bleed Cadbury. We share

the chocolate bars between us. When nothing is left, we
chew the golden foil until callouses grow on our tongues.

We have never seen the stick figure fingers of famine
sneak themselves through the holes in the shut

windows, imploring for a bowlful of rice-starch. But we
have seen its candle-light flame flicker on the window sills,

casting shadows inside our multiplication tables, primers,
school bells and mary jane shoes. We sit down to wrap our

fingers around a ball of rice dipped in fish stew and our
grandmother's butt flaps on the floor in a korai like a

trapped fishtail. Thin bamboo pole in hand. Digging deeper
and deeper into our entrails, lightening the hole in our throats,

>   inventing its own rhythm.

CHRONICLING

The room keeps time: the wall is its familiar. A dust-ridden
photograph hangs above the door. The room is shrinking
but we are still too small to reach into the kinds of screams

that have been assembled into the picture. These fingers we hate,
these arms that won't travel anywhere. Tombur
wishes a new body for herself, and gets it. How,

no one knows. Who grants her, that's a mystery. But
four seconds, a gulp and a gash on her lower lip, an utterance:
wish I had wooden arms that could reach anywhere,

my sister is a wooden frame. A nose like Pinochhio's, a hand
like the mast of a ship. In the story, the ghost-woman
had long arms that could move anywhere while

she remained perched in between the leaves of the sheora
tree: hidden from humans and other ghosts. A bat
flaps through the room, stumbles against the electric bulb

and dies. A drop of blood on the dresser, a drop on the white
pillowcase. My sister prays, standing erect, arms akimbo: arms
like that ghost-woman she wants. So far, only half her wish

has been granted. Wooden fingers which will let her write
everything without forgetting. Mother thwacks her head, followed
by our three aunts, two grandmothers and four great-aunts: *you*

demand too much. Tombur writes down the annals of every
single one of them: these casual slaps. Puts a number, notes
down the time, the date. A list that our mother, grandmother,

aunts and great-aunts wouldn't remember. Only Tombur won't
allow them the privilege of erasure. My sister cannot remember a single
poem written by others: but she can recite the history

of thwacks in this household like a rally-chant, a crimson poem.
A knock with her wooden palm, a demolished photo-frame: inside
a house. A house like a matrushka doll which has lost its capacity to open

deeper. A form of ancestor, whose marrow is melting into ours, whose bones
are rattling against Tombur's wooden arms, still new, still swaying
like a new leaf—untouched by despair. But in the story, the ghost-woman

always vacillated: between ghost and wife, magic and mother. And would always
settle for the latter: *wife, mother*. It is this shame that my sister
wants to survive. It is this shame that my sister wants to outdo.

The shame of never being anything other than half of a ghost-woman.

GENEALOGY

No one ties daughters to doorposts here. No one
severs their heads. Only a grandmother governing

the ways granddaughters should not leave behind
a single grain of uneaten rice. We, the granddaughters, eat

while Zainul Abedin memorizes the streetside corpses inside
our mouths. We know. There are stories floating around—

the neighbor lady who ripped the hole inside her
grandson's throat bigger. With an axe. And other

grandmothers, who supervise their grandkids' meals
with whatever they can find—broomstick, machete, axe or

knife. Our own grandma, twirling only a bamboo, relatively
benign: this is the history that occurs inside the mouth

when you have grandmothers who forever trace
their own footprints in oven-burnt ash.

ASCENSION

Late afternoon and the sparrow releases
an owl-like screech: the house is closing in

tight against the burning neem leaves,
the crows knocking against the window-panes,

the squirrel mother discarding the baby
born blind. With her newly-acquired wooden arms,

Tombur pokes into the corners,
breaks the locks of the boxes. Like babies,

crawling through the emptiness
of adult footsteps, we collect what

can only be resurrected by denying
the height of adult eyes. Crumpled

flags: one red, tattered by rats and termites.
The other, a tri-color national flag, faded

from all the scrubbing. Wrapped
in those flags are hands—bodyless,

severed from the elbows. Hands
that have done what they were meant

to do, made to do. Dirt under fingernails,
no desire to be called back, to be named.

Neither do they want to find spaces
in Tombur's journal entries.

The ceiling fan stops, the room
wrinkles into an old plastic bag.

The hands—bodyless, nameless,
faceless—clutch Tombur's

newly acquired wooden ones.

HISTORY INSIDE OUR MOUTHS

Mother has forgotten to lock up
the history of grandmothers etching riddles on

granddaughters' tongues. This history
of biting tongues we sisters share.

We lick around the edges of the boxes, eat
chocolate bars to heal our tongues. These

tongues sliced by history. We bleed Cadbury,
wishing the boxes open. Mother snores

downstairs. The boxes do not open. Our
grandmother continues to supervise the acquisition of our

tastes. The boxes still do not open. We chew on rice
grains. We dig our teeth in fish fillets. Each a name

of a village. Each a riddle. Our tongues sliced by the effort.
A grandmother with her butt on the korai, a bamboo

pole in between her arms. Threatening
to poke the holes of our throats bigger. Threatening

to de-riddle us girls. We pore over the plates of rice
and fish. Chew on the bones, and dream of breaking open

the locks. This history that happens inside our
mouths. This history that Mother cannot lock up.

II

MAKE-DO MOTHER MYTH

DEFINITION

Mother is a collage of at least three things—a desire to create history, a desire to stay away from history, a desire to be carved into history by others. Like all women who effortlessly recombined these things, she, too, harbored a hole inside. A hole that some preferred to call loneliness. But Mother didn't. Precisely because no one could ever ascribe shapes or colors to it. But this hole had both. And it kept appearing everywhere—in the pillow cover as a hexagonal broken glass, as purple as an untreated bruise. A vermilion square in the middle of the bedsheet. Mother learns to find peace inside the pot of boiling rice.

HEIRLOOM BIRTHSTORY OUR MOTHER REPEATS AGAIN AND AGAIN

A purple bruise on my sister's tongue, mine a size
too small—the footprints of an inheritance that belongs

neither to history, nor to family, nor art. A bus
stumbles against a banyan tree, then a lamp-post,

a beggar woman leaning against it, evaporates. Slowly—
as love leaves a marriage. The bones first, then the skin—she

doesn't have any organs inside. Smear of blood
on the pavement, a finger, a severed toe, a torn sari.

Another beggar woman sweeps the street clean, picks
up the sari, wraps it around her bamboo-thin hips. The thinkable

destiny of an unthinkable keepsake. We arrive,
newborn cries drowned out by the bigger thud of death

outside. This game we would continue to play with each
other—of erasure, impressure, appearance, abandonment. Fists

tightly curled, my gums on Tombur's brows: twins coiled up
together like caterpillars in the same bassinet, trying to eat

each other up. No one thinks of separating our cribs, although
our mother swears, she has heard the two nurses argue: everything is scarce

in the government hospital anyhow. Tombur never opens her fists,
throws them in the air, with every shriek she lets out.

Her protest-rally of one. And I suck my thumb,
hiding it between two fingers: the forever sneak.

When we do not kick each other, we howl as one,
rehearsing ways of renaming ourselves.

TAKING STOCK

Our mother has broken a single word
right through the middle
to name her twin daughters.

Or, so she thinks. A simple truth
slips through her fingernails and crashes
on the mosaic floor, bristles

on my skin like the frills of a starched
navy blue school skirt: my sister
would be the owner of one

syllable more. A syllable more
and a set of conjuncted alphabets.
A moment resembling

bildungsroman: for nothing
can be broken right through
the middle. Not even a word.

BOWS

Our mother hit her head on the wall of our kitchen and you and I watch from the doorway. Yesterday, it was our aunt's turn. These women, who are sisters, took turns dismantling the house and sewing it back together again. You and I roam the alleyways of the atlas they draw with their curse-words and tears. This was before you came back home from school with the knowledge that women were prone to hysteria. Before you began to fold your own bitterness into immaculate paper cranes. You watched, leaning on the door to the room, your limbs indistinguishable from the palisade. Our mother's fingers, now tearing her own hair, uttering the usual predictive impossibilities: *why didn't I kill you two at birth, little demons.* In a minute or two, she would get up, begin to wrap your skinny torso in frills and bows. White lacy bows. Green satin bows. Bows stiff around the edges. Bows with Mickey Mouse faces in the middle. We both knew our mother was painstakingly braiding the emptiness inside. And she happened to name that emptiness *my daughters.* The bows allowed her to give that emptiness a marble glaze. But you were already refusing to be a scotch-taped daughter on the wall. And failing. You were ordered to memorize out loud the multiplication tables all through the night. I wanted to warn you. That our mother, who has grown up on Vidyasagar's morality tales, sprinkled hot mustard oils on erring daughters' eyes. Girls who stopped memorizing lessons. Girls who cannot say no to drooping eyelids. Someone shoved me into mother's metal sewing box. I heard your voice repeating the three times tables again and again. The holler in measured rhythms, the window glasses shattering one by one, covering your hair like unexpected hailstones. And you who can do three things at once: scotch-taped on the wall, truncated and inert, five fingers anchored inside an arithmetic book, the other five, shredding the bows into one hundred and one pieces, threads unspooling at your feet. The house was quiet except for the sound of our father snoring, the rustle of our mothers' fingers on satin and lace, sitting in the living room sewing bows on our dresses. We both dreamt of building a colony of bows, ivory gates. You and I would sit on stools in perfectly black polished red mary janes, legs dangling, selling one-rupee tickets to cow-faced tourists with chartreuse tears and indigo skin.

THE MOTHER WHO READ TOO MUCH

Her life snakes in and out of the blue lines of her daughters'
composition books. She makes them memorize the same
poems that her father once made her learn. The same

multiplication tables, the same grammar exercises. But she
makes them repeat everything seven times over: knowledge
shall bloom inside their little heads like full-grown pumpkin

vines. Our Mother, who has read too much, can take no
chance of failure. Will never take any chance
of failure. We sisters scream multiplication tables

through the neighborhood. Declare them like proclamations
angry manifestoes that our twenty-one year old uncle writes.
The electric poles outside tremble at the sounds of our

memorizing voices. The sparrows forget to chirp, the crows
peck noisily at the window glass, adding to the commotion. A baby
bat forgets its own lessons, unclaws the tree-branches and falls

inside the uncovered manhole: dies. Mother knits,
her hands swinging to the rhythm of our voices.

KITCHEN PASTORAL

Mother lifts up the lid—first her fingers, then her elbows, then her thighs, finally her waist, until her whole body descends into white boiling rice. This she does every morning. Her back bent, she finds safety in the white alley-way. Because Mother taught us to be afraid of everything in her kitchen, I circle around the edges without touching anything. Mother forbade us to step inside the kitchen. Because she was afraid we would melt, like a block of jaggery. Although Tombur insists, I do not pull her out by the waist. Though I want to, I do not know how. Inside the rice-path, our mother's body grows smaller and smaller: small enough to keep haggling with the grocers and vegetable-sellers. In between, she hums Rabindranath's songs. The tunes on her tongue taste like rust. We worry, what if she never comes back? Who would tie our hair into pigtails? Who would make us aloo-bhaji for lunch? Her father, our grandfather, says, *It's nothing. Her love for you has grown too big.* Her older brother, our uncle, says, *Probably she longs for some silence.* But we don't have to worry for long. Once we settle in for an afternoon nap, Mother fans herself back into our midst—into her usual mother-shapeness. She won't walk into her boiling rice-alley again until next morning.

IN BETWEEN

A courtyard is neither a home nor a street.
A threshold to write against

what's inside: walls, dining tables
beds, closets, porcelain tea sets

and the claustrophobia of familiar
faces in every corner.

Faces whose rage-lines we know
too well. From our courtyard, we

can see everything—along
with the potted pepper plantings

they grow on their balconies,
an entire neighborhood of mothers

are shattering.

THE FORTNIGHTLY DOLL FUNERAL

The abundance of wildflower red, holocaust orange in our courtyard—Father leaves the grass to grow. Inside, the house-snake has laid its eggs. From our corner near the window, we can hear the snake-mother breathing. A window in a room is a form of atonement, Mother says. An atonement against the impenetrability of bricks, of the cement that keeps the house together. Our aunt stands behind the door, wiping off the sweet crust of milk and sugar from the baby's lips. Baby does not wriggle its fingers. Baby is a porcelain doll with her father's face, closes its eyes when its head is placed on the pillow. Black eyelashes like arrowheads. This is the twenty-third baby we have buried inside our home in the last eleven months. Aunt keeps pushing them out of her belly. Although none of them ever learns to cry. No one cares about finding them a coffin. Grandmother digs a hole inside the kitchen floor with her shovel and axe, Mother throws the babies in. Uncles clap. Aunt blinks, we're ordered to dance around the hole holding hands. We do, singing *Ring-a-ring-a-roses* at the tops of our voices. This is a song that Aunt taught us. Aunt was a school-marm, before all she wanted to do was to have babies to play with.

BONSAI

In the courtyard of our house, Mother
plants banyan saplings

in ceramic flower pots.
She is forcing rooms on them.

She works hard to keep them small—trims
their leaves, winds wires around them,

tells them which direction
 to bend. Mother's saplings

never outgrow their pots.

FEELINGS

So boring. This singing and dancing and clapping of hands before the babies are thrown in, the hole is shut, the cement replaced as if nothing happened. We know we would be asked to do it again in another two weeks or so. And we keep doing it. Even Tombur never says *no*. Because we want those dolls for ourselves: beautiful miniatures no one allows us to play with.

We both know, a baby-tree, no, a doll-tree is waiting to burst forth from the floor of our kitchen. A tap on the cement, a little digging in: byas. A doll-tree from whose branches dolls are waiting to be shaken free, of course. Dolls with blue marble eyes, pink lips. Dolls with jute curls and porcelain fingers. Abiding time, awaiting to be clawed apart. We need a shovel to let the tree bloom. A shovel to break free the kitchen-floor. A shovel to liberate the expectant dolls, waiting to come to life from the touch of little girl fingernails.

A shovel is what we cannot find. A shovel is what we're not entrusted with. Our aunt never cries. A window is a daub of blood on the wall, Mother says. Aunt is teaching us to find the snake-eggs in the grass: without leaving the room.

BEGINNINGS OF DISOBEDIENCE

My sister is always angry. Here,
with the heaviness of the last night's
rain in between our toes, I repeat

to Tombur what I heard
from grandmother. How in the olden
days girls used the orange shiuli

stalks to dye their saris marigold
yellow. Tombur shakes her head: *no*. Last
night, mother slapped her hard

for stumbling over words
in the national anthem. It is not light
yet, but I know how and where to discern

the lines of that slap on my
sister's cheeks. *Discontented*, Mother
calls her. Mother does not know. Could

not guess. How Tombur holds
another story beneath her skin:
the unseen next. An undevised

rhyme-scheme, the unmemorized
future—waiting to be read. Mother
has prohibited us from leaving our rooms

before sunrise. But here we are.
The air smells of the fumes
from the tannery nearby. A stench

with a capacity to shape-shift—
from dried vomit to sun-simmered
sparrow carcass to mouldy milk. A fetor

even the dewiness of rain and white petals
of monsoon jasmines cannot hide. It is not dawn
yet, and Tombur's hair smells of diesel-smog.

QUOTIDIENNE

Mother is busy wiping off cumin-dust from old photographs, book-spines, the remotest corners of the room. The stories slip away from her palms. Three years old, and we thought, fairies came down to our courtyard at dawn to collect the flowers from the grounds, their dresses sparkling like fireflies. Eight years old, we know: fairies are no one but the children from the slum across the canal. The glinting dabs their kerosene lamps. Picking up flowers to sell. Our maid's daughter Saraswati among them. Mother keeps the ceramic cups she got as wedding-gifts wrapped in white embroidered napkins. We are not allowed to drink out of them. Mother tells us, the past is something she cannot afford to repair.

III

THIS TOWN:
A BROKEN GLASS BANGLE

MORE DISOBEDIENCE

Through the living room windows, we watch the line of trucks and vans that bring the fair to town: rides, folded down like letters. Witch hair: cotton candy. House of Mirrors. Icecream boxes. Freakshows are made of freaks. Freaks riding on wooden boxes, wooden boxes riding on trucks. Toi and Tombur walk. Juju-lady counts. One, two. No one buckles her shoes. Three, four. Toi drags chair, Tombur sneak-opens door.

A BROKEN FAIRYTALE

Our grandfathers did not whittle this city into being. Nor
     our fathers. Or uncles. Neither did the city write itself.

All our men could do was read it: an incomplete
     tableau. Afraid their touch would shatter the city

like an old beetle wing. A broken line on a broken wall.
     Rhythms made unrhythmic through repetition. Clay birds sculpted

into molds. Molds resculpted into clay birds. They
     made ripped rags out of rain-heavy clouds, but did not have

the courage to hang them on poles. When we
     walk into the crevices of this city's shoulder bones,

we do so with the tentativeness of their guilt. Like
     a gash from an axe: lustrous red. A reminder.

Not yet teenagers, we learn this was the price you pay
     when you try to step into the footprints left by fathers.

JUJU-LADY AND CARNIVAL

Juju-lady counts. Puking numbers from her tongue. Juju-lady does not need a pencil and notebook to keep track of numbers. Juju-lady gets up before sunrise every day, and learns her multiplication tables. Juju-lady does not nod, does not take bathroom breaks, does not think of white butterflies while memorizing what she is supposed to memorize. Everyone in the neighborhood can hear her. Juju-lady counts money for freaks. Two rupees to get in, nothing to get out. Juju-lady sells tickets from a high stool, legs dangling from behind her red silk sari. Juju-lady wears hawaii chappals, the heels frayed. The imprints of juju-lady's toes bruising the plastic of the shoes like a cop's fingerclasp. Otherwise, juju-lady is dressed like a bride—red silk sari, red veil, sandalwood paste flowers on the forehead. Juju-lady is the oldest bride we've ever seen. The tree against her back is her bridegroom. Someone dressed the tree in tiny lights—green, red, blue.

OUTSIDE

From our porch to the rail station, the town is a broken glass bangle: sharp on the edges, warped, a rickety rainbow inside. This house is too small for the two of us. Besides, Tombur never learnt to look properly under the bed. I specialize in losing. *Careless*, Mother says. The teachers prefer *unmindful, callous*.

My sister, though, is just stubborn. Says, what is lost is lost. A street is different. Does not demand the touch of our fingers, the meticulousness of sweeping something clean. I cannot ever gather these streets in between my fingers. From the protection of the chair on the porch, I watch the early morning fog—the city transmuted into a very old she-ghost. These oodles and oodles of her white hair.

Tombur says, *gather* is what she is doing in everything she writes and draws. That encyclopedia of ghosts, fairies, elves, aliens and princesses. This dictionary of obscure street names. The patterns she draws and redraws. But she is not moving any closer. A form of learning by heart it is: this gathering. Memorizing. Categorizing.

These things we do to swallow our own fear. Like the houseboy next door. Singing loudly alone at night in the dark attic, keeping the ghosts and spirits at bay. Like us, he is seven. Unlike us, he sleeps alone. Tombur keeps forgetting her lines. We do not have a complete falling-out—my sister and I. Because I do not tell her she was messing up the lines. Drawing them too thick. I do not tell her that, but help her to tear up the deficient ones.

FREAKS

In a freak show, freaks are called by their names. Names from the *Mahabharata*—Amba, Ambika, Ambalika, Arjun, Karna, one by one. One by one they step up. Raise hands and shout *Present Please*. That's what Tombur told me. Only when we walk in a line like a rope—there is no calling of names. Because there is no calling of names, there is no raising of hands. Because there is no raising of hands, there is no one shouting *Presente*. The freaks are *just freaks*. No names. And no roll-calls. No pencils. No check-marks.

A BROKEN PAKSHIRAJ

A horse the size of our teacher's chair in the bush by the canal—wings caught in the branches: flapping. Tombur tries to ride its back, it unburdens itself of her as one gets rid of a mosquito from the wrist. With a flick. She pulls herself up, we sit right beside the bush, laughing. Counting the teeth of the horse, while it struggles to set itself free. In the distance, most of the neighborhood boys are trotting away. Others ride kites: cross the canal. We sit counting the horse's teeth. We do not know what to say to each other. But we know each other: by heart. It's noon, but the canal water is the color of moonless night, reluctant to reflect the sky back. And we sisters learn: staring is its own language. Stare at something anything long enough. Hard enough. It will break apart. As does the horse, its bones scattering over the earth in a rhythm we've never heard before. This is how we learn to locate a sewer-history in stale, silted water, a muck-map waiting to be torched.

SPIDER GIRL

This is a girl who could have been a spider. But is only half a spider. This is a spider who is only half a girl. This is not a fairytale. Neither a metaphor. Nor the moral of a story. But only one of many who are exhibited. Amongst others: a girl with the body of snake, a dog with two heads, a fifteen foot long dead fish in a jar. Without scales, but eyes open, waiting to be plucked. The shit-yellow hue between the white, black and grey of its skin. Twins joined in the bones.

What it means to own. The same shoulders. The same skin. The same belly. The same butt. Same hands. Same legs. Same heart. Same blisters. Same nipples. Same ass. Same hole. Same bones. Same innards. Same toes. Not to be the two parts of a single word. But to be the word itself.

Again, this is not a metaphor. Although twins, we do not share skins. Tombur and I. We are two parts of the same word. Our mother warned us against familiar dangers—strange men, darkness, abandoned homes, sugar and deserted streets. No one warned us against more unified versions of ourselves. No one warned us of the dangers of confronting ourselves as one unbroken word.

BROKEN, BROKEN

Because we cannot infiltrate each others' silences, we hold between
our fingers, two broomsticks. One for each one of us:
Rama and Ravana. Buddhu and Bhutum. Neither
of us ever learnt the meaning of fidelity in stories. The epics

are just starting points. We make the princes go to school
with us. We are setting them to elucidate
our hometown with snot. When they fail, we punish them.
Without any mercy, as one punishes a row of dolls.

INSIDE THE TENT

The wooden boxes are where the freaks live, Sister says, and points to the horizon. She is preparing to tear open the husk of this city and I am still looking for a dream to borrow. So I think of jams and jellies in glass jars. Stashed for others to see. Light the color of lemon rinds the tarpaulin flaps, the crowd of heads. Corners glow like bedside lamps. *It's not lemon, stupid. Shit. Yellow like shit*, she mumbles. But I do not listen. Where I see sun, she sees paper-lantern. When I see *love*, she sees *difficulty*. A slit of sky through the hole: knife-edged. A finger to poke through the hole. Clouds of dust that do not hesitate to throttle. In between our palms: sweat and grease. On the tips of our noses, films of dust. Shards of hair, not ours.

MAGIC, INTERRUPTED

Tombur points to a red satin robe, sequined. A turban pink and purple. A potbelly high as an anthill. That's our Aladdin. Aladdin claps. Sister's arms slip from mine. Before us, the spider-lady waves. The snake-woman folds her arms in a namaskar. The twins blink. The dog with two heads in a magenta tutu does backflips. So much happening all at once, yet this feeling of nothing but the memory of a hole in the air. A hole in which children have disappeared. *Nothing happens by itself*, Tombur whispers, and continues to point.

A push and a shove. The warmth of so many noses breathing together, and a truth flickers on my sister's forehead, wearing nothing—automatic is a myth. Magic is Aladdin opening up his lungs for the spiders to weave a new home. Without the callouses of his hands and the cracks in his voice, this tent would be empty. Because my sister cannot resist looking at the ground, she notices Aladdin's old tyre-plastic shoes. Toenails peeking out. Chapped skin. Unclipped nails. Caked with dry mud. *This is no Aladdin, silly*, sister nudges. This is another example. Of how and where she sees *work*, I see *magic*.

BROKEN, GLUED

Neither of us wants to be a princess. In the books
Tombur reads to me at night, the princesses hardly

possess a line, do not swirl their canoes anywhere.
Do not have bows slung across their backs, do not

sharpen arrow-tips, let alone aim them anywhere.
Otherwise useless, they sleep. Because neither Tombur

nor I can percolate each others' silences with anything
other than slaps, we want to stamp-break

under our heels the fallow repetition of torpor. We
want to *do* things. Rama does things. Ravana does

things. Are therefore protagonists. We do away
with the princesses. In the new play Tombur is writing

I am to be the rainbow. It's easy: all I have to do
is to wear a rainbow suit and do a bridge on stage. *Byas.*

KICKED OUT

In between this ocean and the sky is a rail-station. In between my sister and half-spider half-girl is Aladdin. Jaws clenched, who lifts us up by the scruffs of our necks. This is how we took the kittens by their necks and sat them on terrace railings for the neighbor kids to marvel at. Inside Aladdin's armpits, red satin smells. Jaws clenched, sweat on skin. Jaws clenched, from clapping all day long. Jaws clenched, from faraway rail-stations. Our legs dangle in air. The tips of our mary janes touch other heads. Jaws clenched, Aladdin throws us onto the ground. Outside the tent. Like two used milk bottles. Only this is not a metaphor. We are not milk-bottles. Jaws clenched. We were kicked out because my sister would not quit asking half-spider half-girl her name. With coins stolen from littlest uncle's wallet, jaws clenched, we buy orange popsicles. Jaws clenched. *Let's steal the spider girl tonight.*

BROKEN, MENDED

Because street corners are closed to little girl legends, my sister decides to stare back at this afternoon of imprecise bruises. Last night, it snowed as if it's Siberia. We woke at the sound of snowflakes siring entire cities in the crevices of our gums. The rustle of the shirish in the neighborhood turning into Christmas trees. Icicles like earrings drilling holes in their branches. Unable to fall asleep, we sat on the bed, listening to the mosquito net groan in rhythm along with the trees outside.

A lullaby in irregular rhymes—wordless. Because everyone in this neighborhood shares family histories illuminated by disasters, natural and otherwise, we had fallen back asleep—assured that when some things happen, they happen in the way books have predicted. There is always a book to come home to. An assurance that the ghosts up on the jackfruit tree will be frozen to death in this unprecedented outpouring of white. A proverb that will make ghosts vanish. Yet it is summer. When the night vanishes, the snow, the trees, the lullabies become lines in a long expired election manifesto painted on the wall right outside our window.

Our grandmother, who darns a neighborhood full of women's wounds into slipcovers, says dreams like this can kill without a single drop of blood. But we who know how to sculpt our dreams into moss-green brick walls know otherwise. If these dreams can kill, they can also force open. Force open the windows shut to wind and rustling leaves. The dew-drops on the tips of the grass, a vulture is imprinting the history of this city's bruises on our window-sill—for us to decipher.

STEALING THE SPIDER GIRL

This is a folk-tale in which Tombur steals the half-spider half-girl from the freak show. Sneaks her inside her school satchel. And lets her out in the middle of the rail-station at dawn. Inside Tombur's satchel, half-spider half-girl folds into a paper boat. My sister hides her in between the pages of her composition book. We alternate the bag between our shoulders. Although small and paper like, half-spider half-girl weighs like a dictionary. Needs more than one to carry her around. When we let her out of the bag, she yawns and stretches, clanking her bangles over and above the newspaper boys' rhythmic monotones, the clicking of the chaiwallah's enamel spoon on the tea glass, the whistles of the trains. The morning spills onto us like a frizzy drink from a bottle—Thumbs Up, Limca, Gold Spot—poured into one another. And I notice the details. No silk, only satin. Holes in places, seams coming off. Crude stitches hurriedly done. Colors unmatched. Blue stitched with red threads, red with yellow, yellow with black. The fading purple of her blouse. Skin peeling from the edges of her lips. Smudged kohl on the borders of her eyelashes. Smudged lipstick. Hair in a lizard's tail ponytail. Most of all, what we thought were her tentacles, are torn pages from old newspapers. Seeping ink. *What use can she be put to?* the chaiwallah asks, throwing another spoonful of leaves into the bubbling milk. *We need to know her name,* Tombur says, slipping her fingers through the spider-girl's. It isn't easy, because the half-spider half girl doesn't have any fingers. Only impressions, on a skin as white as the wedding gowns in picture books. We keep asking her her name. Half-spider half-girl laughs. Letting loose her hair from the faded yellow scrunchy, rattling them like metal forks. We decide to take her back to the wooden box in the freak show. *Because, she would be of no use to us.*

OCCUPY THIS THRESHOLD

Hunched over, my sister scribbles a myth bereft of the certainty of slogans, police vans and shootings. To occupy the threshold between love and habit, to leave our own toothbrush bristles in between the cracks of cobblestones, is nothing but our own little girl way of leaving handprints on the dust landscape painted by honking trucks. Hunched over, my sister is rhyming incoherent allegories for a coherent manifesto. A promise to never be a mother. A promise made to no one but one's own self. Her bare foot blisters, oozing pus. We're twins: same size, same height, same width. What we have is friction-love. Hunched over, my sister is assembling a slingshot. The heat morphs the neighborhood houses into a tepid sweat puddle, on the pebbles my sister's sandals: two sizes bigger than mine.

THE SUMMER THAT DEMANDS ITS OWN ALLEGORY

My sister's slingshot breaks the crow's republic up on the electric wire. Death arrives as a scarlet patch on the tip of the mango leaf, a few scattered feathers. The bone-hued dejection of the afternoon, and we sisters repeat the myth in whispers—*here are two suns in the sky above, fighting for our attention*. The woman next door takes down every pot from the cupboard, rearranges them again. Her baby-son giggles, until he turns into a porcelain elf. A week ago, she tried to kill herself—the rope snapped. A sound that reverberated throughout the entire neighborhood. She got up, retied her hair, kissed her little boy on his cheek—the rituals through which a family becomes whole, stays that way for ever. And ever. My sandals stuck in molten asphalt, a puppy barking for the leg it lost under the wheels of a bike—a summer still waiting for its own emblem. Like the spring that burst on these sidewalks demanding young lives a decade and half ago. A spring the call of which our uncles could not ignore. A spring available to us only in metaphors. This is the season when ghosts come to roam the earth to singe their half-frozen skins.

IV

SPECTER HISTORY

THIS IS HOW TOMBUR BECAME A HISTORY TEXTBOOK

A screech of the chalk on the blackboard—the teacher
writes the lessons. The words are measured, like everything
in this room: chairs, tables, books, notebooks,
maps, pencils, globes, assignments, children. Tombur
sits slightly apart from us, leaning on the wall.
Her hands: grabbing onto the words
she has plucked from places in the room: the corner
where the children are made to kneel as punishment,
the teacher's drawer, window-sills, the spiderwebs
circling the ceiling fans, cracks
of the desks where our predecessors
have signed their names
with pencil tips. Her mouth: busy
and full. Chewing on the words
the teacher writes. White
dust collects on her lips
like icicles on windows. Even though none
of us has ever seen an icicle. But we memorize
snow in our classes: it sounds good. Sounds
good to compare
anything white with snow and ice.
Tombur does not have to eat
anything other than words. And vomits
them on demand: in our
teachers' cupped hands, exam notebooks.
My sister cannot avoid
coming first in her classes. Our claps
fill the school courtyard—like forty
empty tin canisters banging against tree trunks.
I shake my head—I am bored
with Tombur's antics. And jealous.
I know what others don't. Three days
old, and she would not stop crying; our mother,
while trying to rock one of her twin
daughters to silence, and if possible, to sleep,

thought to herself, *who knew twins could be so different*;
discovered that this one, that is, Tombur, needs
things other than milk. Just to survive. It began
by her sucking on ink mixed with milk. Then
torn pages. And then whole books. At the dinner table,
our mother would shove pages
down Tombur's throat, folding them
up like ruti wraps. So many thousands of words
inside her toddler veins, and Uncle-Know-It-All
placed his ears on her tummy and confirmed. Chunks
of human history—wars, rebellions, revolutions
and failures—belch inside her. Very soon, she
would give up speaking in her little girl's voice.
Although, on the advice of the pediatrician, she
learned to fake it. All through elementary,
middle, and high school. The heavy histories
would rumble just beneath her squeaky
first girl voice—like the labored breaths
of pneumonia. So eager was Tombur
not to become our mother. They
say: imitation is the sincerest
form of flattery. Wrong. Rejection is.

THE NIGHT OF THE STORM

The storm uprooted the papaya tree last night,
and we celebrated by slapping each other's faces.
Many times. Because together we are an archipelago.
This strain between earth and land. The smell of wet

nayantara petals and rotting dry leaves,
the unsuspected dangers of tangled electric wires.
This push and pull between ocean and earth.
The momentary illumination of lightning

and the thunder: the sky is an angry father
slap-marking the earth. This is a calamity
that resides in the fading bruises of our knees.
The storm yowls: a barking bulldozer, breaking

down the bones of the shiuli tree. The raindrops
on the edges of the gourd-leaves, inaugurating
the year's monsoon and the massacred uncles
come down to roam the earth from their hiding

places inside discarded suitcases. Even ghosts
need embraces, periodic embrocation: of the smell
of wet shiuli in the air, the assurance
of soft little girl skin, the need to train little nieces

looking for new forms to claw in. A future
to sculpt, a present to alphabetize.
We cup our hands, make space
for them to descend, sit, nibble

on bread-crumbs. Our palms become benches
for our ghost uncles. We memorize
the synonymns: *internexion, decimation,*
annihilation, extermination. The friction

of our teeth on tongues. A drop
of blood on each of our tongue-tips,
ghost uncles whisper: *this is what*
remembrance looks like. Restitution, too.

PLAYING HISTORY HOUSE

Uncle so and so taught us that game. Because what cannot be stockpiled inside the museums, must be accumulated inside the hollows of our knuckles. He wasn't a blood uncle. But then, no one was. And we didn't care. Blood is the red thing that oozes out when you accidentally pierce a finger while sharpening pencils. You cannot satisfy the thirst of water with blood. We did not want any uncle-shaped apparitions in our blood. And the real uncles are the ones who fill you up with useless knowledge which you would never be tested on. The knowledge that forever remains beyond the ink-marks of the school examination book. That way, he passed our test. Anyways, that's not the point of this story.

Uncle so and so taught us that game and we played it. Often. Because what cannot be treasured inside the museums, must be written on the roots of our hair. Someone writes a word with the tip of one's fingers on someone else's bare back, you loudly count ten, then you stop for a second and make a guess. Tombur and I play that game with each other. Often. We begin with easy ones. Like *poopoo*. I figure it out and say the word out loud. Then we shout the word to every corner of our terrace until our voices crack. When it's my turn, I write *bastard*. We nibble at each others' heat rashes, popping them with our nails. These letters, etched through the sweat of our skin, daring us to peel off prohibitions: layer after layer. One by one. This was not what uncle so and so had taught us. He used common words. But we do it differently. We try *fuck, fag, sisterfucker* and *asshole*. No one here on this terrace to slap our cheeks. No father. No mother. No aunt. No uncle.

And then Tombur sits up. Takes a deep breath, and scribbles, "Bimalkaku." Although we never met him. He died. Shot. In the swamps. Before we were born. We call him "kaku" anyway. We often used to play Bimalkaku-police amongst ourselves. One of us would run around the terrace and then make a face and fall along the walls. The walls were our alleyways. Just like Mrinal Sen's films. But we don't anymore. Because Tombur, who always has to be the spoil-sport, asked one day, *were there any alleyways and walls in the swamp where Bimalkaku was shot*. None of us knew about that. Anyway, that's not the point of the story. What it is, I write back, "Naxalbari."

Tombur shakes me by the shoulders and yells, "That's not a bad word." I didn't know that. In their home, Bimalkaku's brothers do not hang his picture on the wall. Like they do of those others who are also dead.

AND VOSTOK MEANS EAST

Us children and the dust. The dust and the yellow
book bus. The yellow book bus and the utopia. A
fallen utopia. An irrelevant utopia, an incomprehensible

country. But a book is a book is a book: a red brick
fortress in itself. While other children continue
to play with shiny marbles, Tombur walks inside

a bus-shaped utopia. A utopia that can be folded small,
written on, marked, highlighted, scarred and then ripped
apart. Tombur and I were born within that tearing apart.

We knew that ripping can take many forms: a ritual
visit to an old cemetery, walking thousands and thousands
of miles and recording every little catastrophe

on the way, scratching out old words and making up
new ones. A more literal ripping: splitting a page
of a book from its spine. Uncle so and so says, that's

what he and our other uncles were trying to do when they
were breaking the bones of those statues: tearing out pages
that had long ago been made brittle by rats, devising new

words, making spaces for new writers.

NATURAL HISTORY

On the lines of my sister's palm: the open eyes of a dead sparrow,
the head of a plastic doll. Someone had wiped off the eyes. We know who.
Our next-door neighbor girl—born blind, but can rub off the eyes
of every doll she lays her hands on, without any help
or prompting. Used sanitary napkins: blood-inked
cotton peeping from the thin plastic cover. Broken
eggshells, filled with mud-water and mosquito larvae. Crumpled shampoo
bottles. Soap wraps. A rat, dead, with its mouth open. Stiff.
On the lines of my sister's palm: discarded medicine
bottles. An old radio-box gathering muck. The Murphy
baby still holding on to its milk-bottle. The closed
ink-factory. Broken twigs from a crow's nest, machines
draped in rust and cobwebs, closed iron gates
invaded by weeds. This is the ossuary where we leave
our Five-Year Plans to decompose. On the lines
of my sister's palm: empty cicada shells, an afternoon
of snoring adults. The clandestine rituals of sneaking out,
raindrops on the yellow of the cab bonnet. The sunflower we draw
with the tips of our fingers on the taxi window. The snoring
driver on the seat inside. His sleeping chest, a village-long
usurped land. His elbow, a broken tongue. On the lines of my sister's
palm: the slow shriek of the afternoon coal-train—it won't stop at this
station. On the lines of my sister's palm: the sound
of our neighbor Nitaikaka cleaning his nose before dawn.
The rippling chime of the summer-breeze on the knots of the rope
he used to hang himself in the empty machine-room
of the abandoned factory. Three years after it was closed,
and he, laid-off. On the lines of my sister's palm: anything
that is redundant, lost, superfluous.

OF GHOST UNCLES AND STORMS

On the white of the jasmine petals,
imprints of our mary jane shoes: the rituals
of the morning. And theaters of walking.

In the sparrow's throat: memories
of after-midnight police sirens. The decade
of the vernal transplanted

between leaves glittering
with borrowed sequins
of early monsoon raindrops.

Inside the cuckoo's beak, a repository
of broken wishbones. In between
the veins of the leaves, a staggering,

stammering reminiscence.
Left Right. Left Right. What is preserved
inside museums after having lost

its fangs, teeth and claws.
Some things when assembled, embarrass
 us too much—like unstated, never-stated

death dates, incomplete genealogies. We
leave those out in the open to rot, vanish.
Some things *cannot* be collected, collated

and exhibited, like uncles who died
several years before
you were born, chasing

after ghost-futures. Killed.
And no one in the family dared
to give him a decent funeral.

We do not know his face,
for he does not live in any museum.
Or, for that matter, in photo

albums. Yet he comes back.
That's why he comes back.
To bite our toenails, to touch

 the tips of our fingers. To show
that the smallest places of our bodies
can cower: with fear. Shriek

and bawl in affliction. We hear him
climbing down the attic walls,
like the whirl of a stormy night

wind. We would've ignored him,
but my sister says, she
 cannot leave him to choke

in a box where no one can smell
the slow blood-soaked drip
of the mundane, and everyone

prefers the opacity
of cricket-balls to eyes. Like
other grown-ups, he cannot

be forfeited to loss. Because,
he has already been misplaced
by others. We wait for him

every stormy night—undone,
like a moon on the eve of a full-moon
night. He comes down

to help us
read through
an as yet unpublished primer.

BECAUSE TOMBUR TATTOS VOSTOK ON HER PALM

She is not old enough to snatch
the abrasiveness out of the late afternoon's

palms, the diesel fumes from the plying cars
that settle in between our eyelids,

the shards of a summer sun
pricking our eyeballs.

She walks instead into narrow alleyways as if they
are well-ordered pleats: an eagerness to see

what they can fill her palms with. That is how
my sister begins carving fathomless doorways

into bruised utopias. When she walks inside
the book bus, she carries with her a piece

of our great-aunt's nipples, Bimalkaku's pierced
lungs, and her own hair: torn from its roots.

During nights all my sister wanted to do
was to learn the history of this bruised atlas

the hawk engraves on the bark
of the mango tree. And all our mother

wanted her to do was to learn
by heart the multiplication tables.

TO THRUST BACK

When forced to slip inside the covers of the bed for an afternoon nap, we both speculated as to whether these body-parts could be thrust back, into the frames they came from. But we have never met our great-aunt. No one ever told us her name. And Bimalkaku never came back. Not even as a corpse in a plastic bag at the back of a truck. *We need to find these bodies before anything could be thrust back on them.* This is not something we say out loud. Not even in a whisper. Some things cannot be called to tongue in sounds. But need to be impressed with the tip of our fingernails on the pillows on which we rest our heads, a silent chant in between each others' veins. As for Tombur's hair, she prefers it cropped. Boy short.

ANYTHING THAT IS REDUNDANT

I watch Tombur tiptoe into
this dried up ribbon the neighborhood

calls The River. For a long time, nothing
but a canal. How long, who knows. In these

ripples Bipradas counted the syllables
of his rhyme. Once upon a time.

Inside Tombur's fingers, small bones,
opaque eyes—guppy corpses and mosquito

bites, red as rose petals. An epigraph is what
my sister is after. A commemoration in fragments—

if nothing else, a partial compensation
for anecdotes that cannot be translated

into the language of museums. A pebble
to disturb the ebony quietude, a twig

to rouse the rotten water. The slime
between her toes, the sludge

overtaking her slippers. And Tombur closes
her fist. Closes her fist around perishing

myths: stories which cannot be in anything
other than the color of blood. We both

have memorized the morality behind
such stories—*this is the only way a seedling*

can sprout. What we didn't yet know
were the anecdotes—with or without morality.

There was nothing left
for us to memorize.

CHARACTERIZATION

Ghost Uncle who mocks and argues. Ghost Uncle who never waits. Ghost Uncle who glares. Ghost Uncle who amplifies, multiplies. Ghost Uncle who holds on his thumbnail the entire continent. Ghost Uncle who dreads revisions. Ghost Uncle who collects distant admiration. Ghost Uncle who speaks in translated tongues. Ghost Uncle who walks rejection. Ghost Uncle who is always right.

VOSTOK AND THE LAST HURRAH

I follow my sister, dragging behind
me, with a rope tied around its neck, an
incomplete matrushka doll. Incomplete

because there is nothing inside—no
smaller dolls, no sugar candies, no
thumb-sized little girls. Not even sawdust.

Nothing. Eight years old, and it is within
those wooden hollows of the doll
that I have looked for hibiscus petals

that grow from phantom-limbs: my
version of utopia. For sister, though,
utopia is a pitch-dark alleyway

riddled with ghosts. The lesson that girlhood
summons the demand
for a tongue that would let you taste

the lines in a map. The lesson that to be a girl
is to ask for nose-holes aside from yours—so you can
inhale. A twin-sister who never

shrinks from trailing the streets
into the four walls of the home, is good
enough. Good enough a training ground

for future husbands. A sister, who, offers a wagonful
of freshly sculpted fish gills, resembling
glass shards inside a kaleidoscope—for me

to choose from. I avoid her eyes. The roadside
sound of the breaded eggplant deep-frying in oil,
the dead sparrow in the mouth of the shopkeeper's

broom—almost invisible, and Tombur refuses
to lend me her lungs. Eight years old
and with eyeglasses thick as the bottom of a milk-bottle,

Tombur is already looking for traces
of aridity in the histories of rain. I watch her
walk into that briskness, brusqueness, linger

on the steps of the book-bus. In the wooden
crevices of my matrushka doll, dust-thick
as vermilion, red as rust. This might have been

the moment. This might have been the last
moment when even a scarred utopia
might have nursed too many possibilities.

Like death, the bus hands out a new story everyday.
Tainted, scab-skinned—yet fresh as the rising sun.
My sister has just lost her power to turn them down.

TOMBUR KNOWS THE ROUTE TO MORE UNDERSTANDING

In Ghost Uncle's eyes, shadows of mimeographer's ink-heavy, dye-wet fingertips. On his eyelids sculpted from alphabets, a clandestine printing press. Tombur always knew, a scissor could pick apart his skin, as if he is an origami peacock.

TOMBUR BEGINS TO CHEW ON THE EDGES OF THE CASTAWAY UTOPIA

Inside the catacombs of her thick eyebrows, tiny
train stations with tinier cafeterias. The train
gets heavier and heavier towards Siberia. Little
boys in red fur coats: cherry cheeks. Brothers

entwine their fat fingers in each others' hands. Red fur
coats. Red mittens. Red as traffic lights. Tea boiling
in samovars. Women who have recently graduated

from *maids* to *comrades*, tie their head-scarves
tighter. Beneath the ordered darkness of its shelves,
the bus offers the shelter of old curtains—purple
as unwashed blood-stains.Tombur chews on the edges

of the curtains, the threads unspooling on her shoulders. Like
ants, she feels pulled by the curves of the alphabets—
the sugar that resides in its crevices. Beneath
the metallic shell, the bus offers a pit where

my sister can amass legends. A little girl who plans
to spend her life standing like a stork, a sun which sews
a shirt for the shepherd boys on the ground. Inside
the veins of Tombur's hands, every single detail

becomes a colored glass marble. Her version
of a little girl trinket. My sister chews on the bones
of the alphabets. And with the traces of the marrow
stuck on the chap of her lips, calls back the shadows

of the ghosts who refuse to respond. That's how she
learns to dig through castaway utopias, without spending
even a single paisa. The book-sellers do not mind. It's
already the end of autumn and their buyers are dwindling in numbers.

WHAT GHOST UNCLE TEACHES US

Our Ghost Uncle can never talk to other adults. Whenever he
tries, slogans come pouring forth. With us, the children, he

builds. He moulds clay to sculpt fairy-wings, chisels
raven-bones to make cherub cheeks. Before the night

ends, he learns to speak in little-girl tongues. We recognize—
he is an author of breakages, specters and wraiths.

An author of phantom-futures, with fingers resembling
chisels. With him, we learn how to rip open the walls

of the house we live in. Inside: the stench of the burning
ghat. And yet, the warm aroma of the first cup of tea,

the potato-strips being fried in cumin seeds. Here,
in between these walls, Ghost Uncle tells us,

we will build a museum. A museum of the erased
and insignificant. A museum of the banished characters,

broken plots, mishappenings and abandonments
that my sister has been storing inside her belly.

Sister nods yes, agrees to Ghost Uncle's proposition.
Ghost Uncle rattles his bones like a cymbal: a realization

that we have not yet learnt to place faith in silence.
Our first lesson: never use proper names in your journals.

A state is a state is a state. Fabrication
is the mother of interrogation.

TOMBUR EXPERIENCES THE DWINDLING UTOPIA THAT IS VOSTOK

Very soon, their books dwindle in numbers too. Parenting manuals replace cherry cheek boys, knitting catalogs outpace industrious suns. And Tombur, thick in the history of the alleyway she had dug for herself, finds herself lost. My sister needs to know. Needs to know why the ghosts she is calling forth through her alphabet-induced trances will not reside in the latitudes of her bones.

What is left—her flattened nose on the windowglass, an atlas made of the grease of her skin, a sharpened HB pencil, thin as a needle in between the fingers of her right hand. My sister will draw the ports and towns of the groans, gasps and gulps of the people she will meet, while hiking through the trails of what these morphemes—on their way to gradual obsolescence—have carved.

What Tombur does not know is that I have stolen the last book. The last of the parenting manuals. And tore up its pages to stuff my matrushka doll with. A moment when I avoid being spoken for by my sister.

These simultaneous silences and actions, feroze-blue sequins, cigarette box foils, satin ribbons: this image of myself as a little girl in pressed frocks and bonnets, walking with a parasol under snow-dripping cherry trees. These images I assemble to build my own toolbox, my own unspooled horizon, devoid of ghosts. Mine and mine alone, spliced apart from any interventions of a sister walking too quickly away.

When we reach home, the streetlights are flickering. Half an hour after curfew, Tombur has just begun to gnaw at our father and uncle's silences. Mother breaks the wooden ruler on her knee, for coming home late. If there is a sunset more rhapsodic than this, it must have involved watching the bamboo-castles burn.

GOSSIP

We memorized the morality of the story—*this is the only*
way a seedling can sprout. Ten years old, and, I am tearing apart
a piece of the sky. Straightening it with all of my fingers. Straightening
it and straightening it, rolling it up as poster-paper on which our littlest
uncles would write rally-signs. On its indigo, Tombur has promised
to draw the atlas of our town. Without leaving anything out: thickets
of togor that draw us in, every circus that has ever stopped here, every
beat of the night watchman's stick, every empty booth of every closed down
factory-canteen. Once upon a time. Young men, too eager to trace
their footprints in unfamiliar outlines of blood, had left their homes.
Some were mere boys. Our neighbors remember
their names—Saral, Subir, Bidya. Rathin, Bablu, Biltu. Muzzaffer.
Yet when they remember the years of heralding the vernal,
they do not talk of the boys they knew. They unbutton tales
of an unnamed corpse: cheeks swollen like the belly of a fish,
white and yellow cotton-shirt—wet and torn. Skin white as bone.
Lips and eyes open: what could he see that others didn't? What did
he say that no one wanted to hear? Every neighborhood marked
by its unnamed corpse: whose unnamed corpse did our uncles become?

MAP POINTING AT DAWN

When we tear the petals of polash with the edges of our fingernails,
we are claw-marking our ways into a history of rust, from which

little girls are to be kept buttoned up. A night-storm carves
the polash-petals, manipulating the effulgence of a bruised

sun to crimson. Ghost Uncle is a calligrapher
who cannot hold a pen between his fingers. This is just a sentence

in this history of rust into which we are trying to creep. This
history of crimson petals illustrated with upturned nails, secret rooms

at the back of a police station: interrogation. But Ghost Uncle
is sculpting a polash: chiseling it out of the threads of a flag torn

right through the middle. Alive, this would have been nothing
but painful. Dead, his nailless fingers are adze-sharp. My sister

is chewing on her fingernails, and will continue to chew until it hurts.
When her cuticles begin to bleed, Ghost Uncle buys her a globe.

From then on, they spend the early mornings together, counting
the unnamed graves in our backyard. If I learn anything by observing

them, it is this: not all flowers can be folded into origami
cranes. Not all flowers can be chased out of their ghosts

simply through the memorization of craft and diligence.

LESSON LEARNT

Because Tombur wants to draw within an atlas
every mark left by rising water, every trail carved by every
spider, she spends her afternoons outlining
her pencils around the memories of that unnamed corpse:

two lines for the canal, three for the bridge. Trees,
stick figures in green. Where in the vanished water
to build the dead? Where in this muck to write
his gravestone? We know their names. Our neighbors

remember them. What we do not know are the stories
of *why* and *how*: stowed away, eclipsed, shrouded
between the notes and rhythms of maimed music.
We learn quickly—Tombur and I. That offerings of blood

do not suffice for the saplings to take root.

THE BEGINNING OF A FALLOUT

Tombur learns something about Ghost Uncle. That when he attends the barbed-wires around the borders of an atlas, he forgets what is dainty. He lets loose his rolls of papers across the storm-soft mud and points out: exquisite blisters embroidered on satin home-stitched wings. Ghost Uncle says, addressing both of us together, *this is what the unseen is made of.* He teaches Tombur to separate the scar from the sequins. I stand apart. My tongue slips over the words Tombur and Ghost Uncle are together building a cadence with. Tombur looks at me from the corner of her eye, and sticks out her tongue.

THE QUEST, THE HISTORICIZING, THE ARCHIVING

We do not know what it feels to dig our toes in mud that grows.
We do not know what it feels to find our own faces in water

that does not wound. We both have heard the ballads: how
in not-so-far off villages, where the crow's claw land stealths

into the saline water, women know how to blow brooms
into scythes. A clap of their hands, one long ululation: tangi leke hamla bol

A chorus of their stomping feet, a storm would blow
the hyacinth-roots towards the zamindar's house: sarki leke hamla bol

The refrain echoes in the work songs whose rhythms
they use to husk rice

                                        hamla bol   hamla bol

The names of those killed, they weave
into quilts used to keep themselves warm.

But those are just that. Stories. Inside the soles
of our shoes, we have the secret: we do not know

what it feels to hold the rice saplings in our own fingers.

ANOTHER LESSON LEARNT

Today Ghost Uncle is unfolding and folding papers that other adults have tossed out. An owl screeches past his head, circles over ours. Ghost Uncle doesn't even look up. We watch him fold the papers from our old drawing books into shapes: cranes, ships, paper lanterns. Both of us hope his shapes will mutate into little fairies. Instead, what is left are complicated alphabets which require rigorous sharpening. So monotonous that I could not be let in. And even Tombur, who speaks in an adult voice, can only limp among them. A feeling inside her: that she has lost her toes. But it is while trying to walk amongst the denseness of these alphabets that Tombur learns the cost of always speaking in the adult voice of a book.

FOR US,

        this river dried into a canal into a string.
        For us, this closed ink-factory. Machines
        draped in rust and cobwebs, closed iron
        gates invaded by weeds. For us, this sewage water
        and its storehouse of unnamed corpses.

        For us, this broken bridge: a step
        at a time. For us, this parchment paper,
        pieces of the sky, pencils and this knowledge—
        offerings of blood do *not* suffice
        for the seedlings to bud. For us,

all the time on our fingertips, while the neighborhood
    boys gallop away. For us, the swishing
        sounds of them riding
    their kites. For us, this staying behind. For us,
this afternoon of snoring adults. For us, Tombur giving
    stories to the unnamed corpse. This closing

        of our fists around things
        others would simply throw out: glass
        shards from window panes, a shred
        or two of the scarlet kites the boys
        are riding. For us, this

    solitary eyelash on palm, this whispering
    of a wish: *maim them*. Maim those
    things, make them forget how to draw
    blood from skin, set them to the task

        of unstoring locked mysteries.

V

CAUSELESS CATASTROPHES

THESIS, ANTI-THESIS AND NOTHING MORE

Around here, trainwrecks are written about how deeply dumplings are fried in oil. Homes are mapped along the black spots of a freshly-fried shingara. On my palm, a newspaper bag of jilipis, awkwardly balanced. A crow circles above my head: sugar always invites the undesirable. I lick from the smallest pore of my cuticles the dripping syrup. Standing alone on the sidewalk, I watch my sister shake off the stink of a summer sun from her shoulders. These red ants between my toes and slippers: how even when I think I am alone, I am not.

A chameleon turns the shade of a betel-juice stained wall: the swollen pouch of red on its neck, which we think of as our blood. Sucked out of our eyes. I refuse to share with Tombur my jilipis. Grandmother sits on the porch, sucking on a mango. Curses us: *badmaish maiya duikhan*. Still oblivious to the real history of the unknotting of her sari-end. The emptiness inside. Who stole the ten rupee bill, and how. The relationship between these jilipis, that ten rupee bill and the loose, empty ends of her sari. Slaps Tombur. Tombur yells back—*Witch! Why don't you die?*

WHAT TOMBUR THINKS ABOUT ORAL CULTURE

Tombur does not do talk-stories because she finds repetition horrifying. And that is all there is to talk-stories: repetitions. Grandmothers do talk-stories. And repeat. Things you've heard four thousand and seventy-six and ninety-nine times. Mothers hit their heads on the walls finding the same faults with the same fathers. Although no one listens to them, neither do those fathers change. Ever. That, too, is a kind of talk-story. *The useless kind though*, Tombur says to me. Digging her index finger deep into her nose-hole. She is trying to find the story she wants to write deep within her own marrow. Tombur does not do talk-stories. She writes. Says, she wants her stories to fly beyond the walls of this home, this courtyard with guava trees, this street with too many madmen and stray dogs. Says, she wants her stories to rustle on the bones of those whose names she does not know. Will not ever know. I try to convince my sister. *Hearing the same story makes it impossible to forget.* This isn't something I have decided on my own. But this is what our great-aunt says. Tombur shakes her head *no. You repeat things when you've nothing new to narrate.*

SPACE FOR ONE

There is always just enough space for one errant
little girl to be left alone. Left alone to illustrate

her own book with the debris she gathers
from the sidewalks. Left alone to chase

the paper-shards she has torn from the posters
on the walls. For the rest of us, this is it: a slow

anthologization of suppressed howls. Suppressed,
transmuted into carcasses. Of half-accomplished

rebellions. Like other little girls in this hamlet,
I am learning to survive. Survive in the crevices

of half-deeds. Too much sugar between
my fingernails. Too much sugar and memories

of wounds pried open—the fresh smell of turpentine,
the sawdust, the flies resting on the

pastries inside the glass showcase of the first ever
Jalojog in this part of the town. The smell

of a pincode that can only be traversed by electric
trains, of how desire is nothing other than the greasy

noseprint of a child on the glass-door of a shop. Once
upon a time, Mother told us a story how a little

girl's tummy would not stop honking like a car.
That's what happens when you can't stop eating

what's sold in the streets. Four years old, and we
already know a cautionary tale is nothing but a

prohibition. A five rupee bill inside my palm—sweaty,
edges frayed, yet a gateway to syrup-utopia.

Stolen from the knot in our grandmother's sari
when she was sleeping—mouth open. This is

the kind of rebellion I excel in—half, silent.
Tombur would've argued. Would've attempted

to remake the sequence. Would've been
slapped, would've slapped back. I am still

following Tombur's every footstep. But, I
am tired of writing down everything she says.

FEARS

There are quite a few things that I need to know if I have to be that perfect girl. A long list of things to like. A long list of things to be: dainty, pretty, pink handbag, knee-length silk frock, a green-bead necklace. Tombur sneak-reads my list, frowns and says, *Be afraid!* I don't know how to be alarmed. Or whether I should be at all. Or not. But some of those things I already like. Only if there was no Tombur. Inside my little book, I make a list. Add an item to it everyday. No one knows this is why it takes me so long in the bathroom. I am young, but not young enough to not know there are crevices in your body. Crevices in your body where even a twin sister cannot reach. In those interstices, I store my little girl desires: unassailable, tended and articulated.

MY LADYBIRD BOOKS LITTLE GIRL DESIRES

A door painted
the color of ripe lemons, a
watermelon
rotting properly.
Immaculately shaped
bangs on foreheads. Mary Jane
shoes—red. Socks that stop
at the edge
of your knees.
In noncommittal colors
of boiled potatoes
and rice. Alice in Wonderland
dress sleeves. Ankle-length
skirts. Frills on
the necklines. Dupattas
with sequins. Waist-long
hair. A conch sharp
nose. Fuchsia nail-polish.
Peacock blue
silk bow. Glass
bangles the shade
of rainbow. Rhinestone
bindis to match
every skirt
that billows out
like an angry monsoon
season mountain stream.
Mickey Mouse
applique; Peter Pan
collar. Purple
seams, indigo
lace. Butter dye
skin.

CREATING DOLL-MOLDS

We shut Saraswati—our maid-servant's daughter—in the old trunk in the attic. She is asking too many questions about the poem we are making her memorize. With every one of her questions, the pages in her textbook are unraveling. We cannot have that.

Tombur laughs. We had taught dolls before, making them sit in a row. Had spanked them with the wooden ruler when they failed to deliver.

Here, we molded another girl into a doll.

A DOLL

is a body strapped too loose inside my old purple-and-white polyester dress. A doll is the fabric wrinkled at the edges. A doll is skin chapped and rough like the bricks of an old, crumbling wall. A doll is the aura of our mother's benevolence wrapped around her bones. A doll is hair doused with coconut oil, a face broken into shapeless cracks. A doll is a tight pony-tail held back with a red nylon ribbon, faux leather sandals.

A doll is a body we can bruise while playing with. A doll is a face we can hurt without any remorse.

A CHILD IS TO BE SEEN NOT HEARD

A little girl even more so.

Tombur gorges on books, learns
      to speak back to the adults in borrowed languages.

I am mastering the art
      of becoming a trinket. A cantata of well-pressed

satin-frills, a recognizable montage of hairclips
      and well-combed child hair. A compensation: always.

For the sister who has not yet learnt
      well the little girl songs. A compensation

      for that disgrace. I make my mother proud.
           A twirl of my red satin skirt, and Mother

      knows: she can breathe. She can breathe
           a sigh of relief. A cliché that is,

      but true. Nevertheless. She has learnt. Imperfectly
           as it is, this science of embroidering a daughter.

      Mother does not know. Those who devised
           proverbs did not know. This child, who

      can be seen, can also see herself. From the daintiness
           of bows, barrettes and buttons, I stare.

BETWEEN TOMBUR AND SARASWATI

My sister, her head so full of borrowed stories, eager
to chew up the world—in broken tongues. This other

girl, so bereft of stories, waits to be sculpted
in Tombur's flawless literacies. Saraswati offers

Tombur her patient tongue, hollow ribcage. Her shoulder
blades sharp—cartilage-like. Eyes without

eyelashes—unblinking, spotted like a parrot's.
The stench of the mole-droppings around us,

held fast by unopened windows, cockroach-wings
in our hairs—brittle as dried petals. Insect eggs

inside the cracks of the spines of the old fifth-grade Bengali
textbooks, a mosquito caught in the cobweb: Tombur is ripping

apart the plotlines for Saraswati—an imitation
of what her teachers do for her. Saraswati sneezes.

WHAT I SEE WHEN I STARE

My oldest aunt, gourd-vines
in place of limbs. Her
mother-voice
labeling details for my
cousin: *this is how
you knead a dough into a national flag.*
My oldest great-aunt
decorating the terrace
with pickle-jars. Green mangoes
on yellow mustard
oil, red chiles, lemon
pieces, turmeric dust.
Approaching the rising sun
with a pragmatism that borders
on violence; pickle bottles
under her armpits, great-aunt
chases the sun until he
sits still on our rooftop, dangling
his red-shoed legs.
The great-aunt's sister,
who, when mango pieces
were not enough, had
ordered her daughters
to cut off their toes
and put them in the mason
jar to wilt. That's the story
our grandmother loves to repeat.
A neighborhood
of grandmothers and great-aunts
pickling their own skins. A
community of aunts
whose hair smells
of onions and goat meat. A
colony of mothers who
carry kitchens on their skins. Our
own mother. The shrimp-peel,

dry and transparent sticking
on her fingertips. And she herself,
shrinking with every one
of our bites on her
stuffed pumpkin leaves.

THE PLOTLINE OF THE POEM TOMBUR EXPLAINS TO SARASWATI

Once there was a king—not so good. Because he wasn't that good, the huts were to be burned. All of them. That was his order. Those huts that belonged to the farmers, the craftsmen, the masses, the crowd, the hordes, the multitudes. But what is most important is the fact that by the end of the poem, the king went through a change of heart. He rebuilt the huts he had burnt.

WHERE MOTHER'S STITCHES FAIL

All of Mother's stitches feel imperfect. Tombur roams the house like a seam hanging loose. In old overalls, denim boys' trousers, matted hair. Falling apart. Croaking unfamiliar stories in her alphabet voice. And Mother does not know how to tuck her in.

I make it up. By being the real little girl that my sister never will be.

SARASWATI'S TRANSMUTATION

Saraswati should have continued to memorize, until the poem becomes words inside an old government file, yellowing overhead. But she moves her books away, cleans her fingers of book dust and raises her eyes to meet my sister's, asking: *Where did those folks live while the king was rebuilding their huts?* That also happens to be the time—when Saraswati tries to scratch scars on our bodies.

Her servant-daughter's fingers, thin like bristles mutating into claws, gashing into the poem, the alphabets, the cockroach wings, Tombur's eyes. That is what it is like to try to become a bear—possibly, probably. Vociferously.

IN MY NOONDAY DREAMS,

Tombur becomes a book: her limbs
and legs the covers, her skeleton
the spine and her bones the pages.

There is nothing wrong with that.
The question is, what kind of book
my sister is. From my side

of the bed—Tombur sleeping
with her cheeks on the palm,
the old madhubani print sheet

covering half of her drooling
face—is the kind that's dense.
Full of small small writings.

                    No pictures.

HOW WE GET EVEN WITH SARASWATI

But we who owned teddy bears in multicolored
multitudes, we of the flawless literacies, we who

knew how to cup our lips around words, also
knew how to turn a growling bear into a porcelain

bird. The immaculate verbosity that can be unraveled
only in front of servant-girls—*how are we supposed to know?*

*Did we write the poem? What you're asking won't be
there on the test. Stupid girl!* Our hands: tentacles, shucking

off innocence, squeezing her into a blanket. Foldable.
And we shove her into the old trunk in the attic,

close the lid. Inside the rectangular darkness
of the trunk: dust, our father's old college textbooks,

mother's old diaries, notebooks, old newspapers. Myths,
private histories, facts. The memory of her skin

on our palms: scaly like braided coconut fibre. The memory
of her elbows: pin-sharp, the sound of her bones snapping,

impelled in the holes of our pierced earlobes long after we shut
her in. We are on the verge of gifting this house its first real ghost.

According to Tombur,

first of all, once upon a time blah blah blah that's not a story.

5 X 3 = 15, now that's a story.

Second of all, a book is a house. The pages its walls. The alphabets its windows. The sentences doors. Not all houses are homes. Not all books can become your home. But some do. Are. And they open their walls for you to scribble on.

THE FIRST REAL FALLOUT

A disagreement with my sister about what a book is,
the cacophony of harmoniums throughout

the neighborhood. It rained last night, the wood has
grown. My index finger on the keys, a tuneless *sa*

and an epiphany: inside its wooden chasms, what
the instrument hosts is a family of cockroaches. On

the tips of my fingers are specks of wood dust—crushed,
white fluorescent light. It is not yet light outside,

and the neighborhood is beginning to be owned
by little girl voices. A cloud-like shadow over the houses,

and the keys are coming off on my palms. All little girls
are taught the same seven songs. The same notes, and the neem

leaves outside are choking on them. I know more than seven. I
press the keys harder and harder. Pump with a pace

that approximates the boatman's oar battling a storm.
The keys come off with every nudge

of my fingers—bones from an untrodden
graveyard. I blast out a song

from the box. It's true that my sister has broken
my harmonium before. Revenge for disagreement

over what *behenchod* means. But I who know
more than seven customary songs, have something

to teach my sister. And this is what I tell her
without my voice shaking. *A book is not a house.*

It is a graveyard.

Mutation

We forget that we have shut Saraswati inside the trunk. It is nothing but an error. Like the words we are ordered to speak and write in English: spelt perfectly, but misspoken often. We do remember though: an hour later. And rush to the attic to lift open the lid. No Saraswati inside. But a sparrow. Hungry for grain. Poking holes inside the pages of the books.

THE ONLY THING THAT STILL BINDS US TOGETHER

is Saraswati. We watch: assured. Put the sparrow on our palms. So elegant, so fragile. We stroke its feathers: it shits right on our fingertips. That too, warm and yielding. We let it go. Sing in unison: *flutter, little sparrow*. Begin to plan on a method. How to steal this thing that she has. But we don't.

A BOOK IS A GRAVEYARD

which needs to be dug in. Periodically.
The bones retrieved and the dead nudged

to talk. A book is nothing but a conversation
with the dead. Ghosts do not know how to rest

in peace. Neither do books. Sister does not mind
setting up a tent inside a graveyard. As it is, she

likes conversing with the dead much better
than the company of other little girls. These days, me and Tombur

hardly speak. Yes, we have gifted this room,
this attic, this house its first ever child-ghost.

And Ghost Uncle stops visiting us. The museum
we planned to build together, remains unbuilt.

I TRY TO FIND MY SISTER'S HOME

When inside a book, I try to find my sister's home. Because that is her diktat. What I find: a shiuli tree, an iron gate, a porcelain house. Two women push a bucket of water and a wet rag between them. This rag, was once our mother's sari. Like soldiers—unsmiling and symmetrical, their fingertips smell of phenyl. A woman clicks open the iron-gate: she sews the other woman together.

That woman happens to be Saraswati's mother. Saraswati never comes back. Neither as a sparrow-bird, nor as a human. But her mother keeps coming.

Every day, the cleaning. In every room, the minor histories of common collapse. The neatly stitched curtains, the rows of spotless china teacups, the living room almirah, family pictures no one looks at anymore.

I put my ears on the wall, intent for the sounds of my sister's footsteps. If nothing, at least echoes. Still, nothing. No sister. No sistersong. Nothing.

But there are composition books everywhere—on shelves, on floors, in the cracks between couches. I haul one out, write my sister's name again and again. A form of howling. A form of chanting. A form of looking out for each other. Over and over, until my sister's name becomes lines handed out by teachers. As punishments.

V

A BRIEF HISTORY OF CLAMOR

TEACHING THIS SYLLABIC LANDSCAPE TO DANCE

Like a cabinet, a goddess is crafted: like this city whittling its own little girls. Satin the color of car fumes, pleats acerbic against the hair in our armpits, elbows and knees. A bruise on the shiuli petal stuck in the mud, its orange stem upturned, the imprints of a car tyre on the knee-caps of my sister. There is a poem hidden inside this lump of clay, in hands that bend silt into immaculately chiseled cheeks. We do have a word reserved for potters who formulate loam into divine. What we do not have is a word for little girls who want to store that knowledge in discarded matchboxes.

In the raven's beak, this knowledge, absconding. In the fingers of every artisan, memoirs of necessary defilement—how the mundane is indented on the faces of the goddesses we make. A starlet rode by on her bike yesterday: past the dried canal, the carcasses of the cars, rows of abandoned factory gates. There was no reason for us to know this. But her wheels got stuck in the razor-thin cracks of the cobblestones. Her ghagra flowing like the petals of hibiscus: purple silk, intricate thread birds. Alabaster face, gossamer arms. Every one of us memorized her, bit by bit. A little at a time. And she vanished. Vanished under the pressure of our eyelids, became the steam in our grandmother's teacup.

Where she vanished, we don't know. And don't want to know. But our goddesses are to be schooled. Schooled in stamping a face on clay, to impress on divinity what is mortal. This is also how we ghost our goddesses, insert our own fingers in the distance between the dead and the divine, make dolls of their clay limbs. Last year, it happened to be the dead queen from a far-off land. This year, the vanished actress. In the courtyard, my sister is skinning sparrows. She is done with nineteen of them: eighty nine remain to be peeled. Drums are to be fashioned out of dead sparrow skin. A step forward in schooling the goddesses we worship: how and when to make space for the demons they kill as ritual marks. *Beauty is nothing but the shadow of a blood-drop on a needle-tip*, says the neighborhood madman. A blur, a sound, a rhythm: *do or die*.

Do. Do. Do. Die. Die. Die. The taste of ash on my tongue. Fire in between their teeth, our littlest uncles— no blood relatives to us—are dancing. Dancing to repossess the dead. The lion-shaped ebony clouds on the horizon, the upturned umbrellas of the passersby, the flapping tops of the coconut trees—I am watching the storm from the protection of the living room window. Outside, with newspaper shards, broken twigs and ripped polythene bags thrashing about, Tombur, thick as a myth, is letting loose her banyan root hair. She swallows a whole hornets nest—with the insects intact inside—and does not even burp. I am scared of norwesters and sister shouts. Shouts an order: *quit painting those damn toadstools blue*. A day ago, our grandmother threw away a bowlful of Maggi noodles, thinking they were overgrown maggots. Tombur sat near the dumpster picking them up, wrapping them on her fingers like threads—one by one. We are learning to wrest our fingers on what is slippery. Sister has just begun to let the crows nest inside her curls.

Me, Toi, on my way to a cryptic closure—fishhooked inside a rosewood box, a hyacinth purple skirt to twirl. Here, in the middle of our courtyard, a face is what my sister sculpts for me—a sharp half-moon, scythe-shaped. Like obsolete poems. I watch through the keyhole. Dust in her hair, dust on her tongue, hands spread. My sister is dancing with our uncles, the summer storm between her fingertips. She is chewing its brown feathers alive. It was our twelfth birthday yesterday, and in the pages of her notebook, new resolutions: *a book a day keeps everyone away. Make the rail-station as much of a home as these rooms*. But what is more, Tombur has resolved, never to be anything older than eleven.

A new ritual mark: this is how fair-skinned goddesses learn to make space for demons they had once been taught to kill. My sister is learning to befriend whatever the goddesses were meant to kill—a darkness that resembles the raven's feathers, a blue that echoes the starlit sky. This is how this city whittles its own little girls, and we let her.

NOTES

1. The names of the twins in this book—"Toi" and "Tombur"—are derived from a Bangla/Bengali word *toitombur* which means, *full to the brim*.

2. **"Historying This Syllabic Landscape":** This poem has been inspired, amongst many things, by poems of Agha Shahid Ali and Sarah Gorham.

   Consequently, the lines "A story of a young man's shriek in every tip of a leaf,/ drippings of a suspended tire on an eighteen year old's back: *Naxalbari is not the name of a village only*" are almost verbatim reproductions of Agha Shahid Ali's lines from his poem "I See Kashmir from New Delhi at Midnight," "Drippings from a suspended burning tire/ Are falling on the back of a prisoner,/ the naked boy screaming, 'I know nothing.'"

   Ali's line appears in italics in my poem as a marker, amongst many things, of the current Indian occupation of Kashmir. As a holder of Indian passport, who also supports Kashmir's right to self-determination, I want to use Ali's lines as a mark of my solidarity to the Kashmiri struggle. Yet, that solidarity is precarious, precisely because my use of these lines—by a Kashmiri-American poet—possesses the danger of replicating that very same occupation I am speaking against. Hence, this very inadequate method of italicization.

   The lines "A five paisa coin thrust/ between her slitted lips, blue-bead eyes deboned,/ her plastic skin pockmarked with ink-stains, on the forehead/ an oversized bindi stolen from the aunt's dressing-table drawer:/ the doll's head is an uncharted city" grew out of my repeated and obsessive readings of Sarah Gorham's poem " Bust of a Young Girl in the Snow." These lines carry in them the memories of Gorham's lines: "Lips apart, ear split/ oyster, rough erosion/ crawling up her nape/ and, over the cheek, a verdigris birthmark."

   The lines "Scraps of history on the little girls' eyelids, their boycut hair, scars on the chins and/ weeping lips. Memories that love to poke. The tips of a wound, an incision right on the skin", similarly, are rewritings of Gorham's original lines, "They accumulate/ on the child's brow,/ her bowl-cropped hair,/ tarnished dimple and fold/ of neckskin."

Similarly, the line "cow licking its dead calf" is an almost verbatim variation of a line by Sarah Gorham, "a cow nudging its dead calf."

3. The coinage "Make-Do Mother Myth" that has been used as a title of Section II is a nod to Ching-In Chen's formulation "Makeshift Family Myth" in her book *The Heart's Traffic*.

4. **"Heirloom Birthstory That Our Mother Repeats Again and Again"** has been inspired by Sara Tracey's poem "Two Wombs" and takes one of its central images as its starting point. The lines, "We arrive,/ newborn cries drowned out by the bigger thud of death/ outside. This game we would continue to play with each/ other—of erasure, impressure, appearance, abandonment. Fists/ tightly curled, my gums on Tombur's brows: twins coiled up/ together like caterpillars in the same bassinet, trying to eat/ each other up. No one thinks of separating our cribs, although/ our mother swears, she has heard the two nurses argue: everything is scarce/ in the government hospital anyhow" are rewritings of Tracey's lines, "We were so small,/ the nurses put us in one crib like twins. Our mothers/ found us holding hands, foreheads pressed together/ as if telling secrets. When they took us home,/ we wouldn't sleep apart. By Thanksgiving,/ Aunt Jill was living on the couch, Stella and I/ curled like spoons in the same bassinet."

5. The poem **"Kitchen Pastoral"** takes one of its central images from the poem "Rannaghar"/ "Kitchen" by Sanjukta Bandyopadhyay, which, in itself, engages in a meta-textual writing of Sylvia Plath's suicide as one of its central themes.

The line "Her father, our grandfather, says, *It's nothing. Her love for you has grown too big*" quotes the lines "I've decided it is a sweetness no one deserves, her love/ for us grown too large, like the oversized heart ever expanding" from Julianna Baggott's poem "How It Begins."

6. **"Bows"**: This poem developed out an engagement with the essay "On Daughtertantrums," by Carina Finn. I am especially intrigued by Finn's observation that "What Chelsey Minnis, Lana del Rey, and Jennifer Tamayo all have in common is an adoration for daughterly aesthetics coupled with a total disdain for the concept of parentage, and the knowledge that one cannot really escape it. The perpetual daughter gets stuck in loop because she does not want to give up her bows, she wants more bows, and wearing bows indefinitely throughout time time is an exercise of agency in a faulty system." (http://montevidayo.com/2012/08/on-daughtertantrums/). The poem developed out of a simultaneous agreement and disagreement with the statement, and can be read as engaging in a creative-political debate with such. My poem celebrates the knowledge that "an exercise of agency in a faulty system" is way-too-limited to begin with. It is that "faulty system" that needs to be smashed to pieces. The smashing begins with the tearing up of the bows.

7. **"The Mother Who Has Read Too Much"**: The first line of the poem is a riffing off of Kristy Bowen's line "Her life/ eddies and pools in the hollows of her/ bedroom."

8. **"In Between"**: The lines "the claustrophobia/ of familiar faces in every corner" have been inspired by the lines "It makes all the difference/ to see, at every turn,/ a familiar face" in the poem "New Tenants" by Renee Emerson, and have been written as a variation of the original lines.

9. **"Playing History House"** was inspired by the poem "June 29, 1968 (from *Rocket Fantastic*) by Gabrielle Calvocoressi. My poem is a response to Calvocoressi's original poem, and uses her poem as a kind of tribute-shell, to articulate a very different, yet similar story. The first line of the poem "Uncle so-and-so taught us that game" is a straightforward tribute and response to Calvocoressi's line "Did we ever teach you that game?" My subsequent lines "Someone writes a word with the tip of one's fingers on someone else's bare back, you loudly count ten, then you stop for a second and make a guess. Tombur and I play that game with each other. Often. We begin with easy ones. Like *poopoo*. I figure it out and say the word out loud." are variations of Calvocoressi's lines "You say a name and then you shut

your eyes/ And spin and spin together and then you/ Stop and look up and have to find/ It is in the sky. The first one to find theirs/ Gets a point. You start with the Greek/ Names because they're easy to find."

The title of the poem and the phrase "History House" were taken from a coinage by Arundhati Roy in her novel *The God of Small Things*.

10. **Vostok** refers to Vostok Publications, Kolkata, a publishing house which used to publish the Bengali editions of Soviet books. Throughout the 80s and early 90s, Vostok also ran book-mobiles, which sold books and worked as community reading spaces for many neighborhoods in and around Kolkata.

11. **Ghost Uncle:** Ghost Uncle is dead, obviously. Ghost Uncle was also a left political radical, who, like the many young men and women of his generation, was killed by the police in 1973 in an "encounter" after severe torture in West Bengal, India. Ghost Uncle's memory cannot, by any means, be separated from the memories of the Naxalbari uprising in India.

12. **"Of Ghost Uncles And Storms"** has been inspired, partially, by Brenda Mann Hammack's poem "Museum", and variations, echoes and essence of Hammack's lines "Some things we don't mean to collect,/ like ailments and disappointments" keep appearing throughout this and other Ghost Uncle poems. An obvious variation of Hammack's lines are my lines: "Some things when assembled, embarrass/ us too much—like unstated, never-stated death dates, incomplete genealogies." As such, Hammack's ghosts, as they appear in her book *Humbug: A Neo-Victorian Fantasy in Verse*, have played an extremely important role in the figuration of my ghosts.

    Also, my line "Like/ other grown-ups, he cannot be forfeited to loss" is a response to Hammack's line "She, therefore, leaves the grown-ups to perdition."

13. **"Anything That Is Redundant":** The lines "In these/ ripples Bipradas counted/ the syllables/ of his rhyme" are variations of the lines "Into your murmuring waters, Rizal's moon once spilled his verse" by Barbara Jane Reyes.

Also, Reyes' lines "I've seen the first seedlings/ sprout, fed by these offerings of blood" appear in this poem and a few others in this section, as an insistent shadow, with which my poems often wrestle and argue.

14. **"Gossip"**: Saral, Subir and Bidya are the names of three young men killed in police "encounters" during the historic Naxalbari uprising in West Bengal, India in the late 1960s and 1970s.

15. **"The Quest, The Historicizing, The Archiving"**: This poem, amongst other things, is a nod to Chris Abani's TED Talk, "On Humanity."

16. **"My Little Girl Desires"** is a semi-cento glued together out of lines by Tarfia Faizullah, Renee Emerson and fragments from my own juvenilia.

17. In **"Thesis, Anti-Thesis And Nothing More"** the lines " On my palm, a newspaper bag of jilipis, awkwardly balanced. A crow circles above my head: sugar always invites the undesirable. I lick from the smallest pore of my cuticles the dripping syrup. Standing alone in the sidewalk, I watch my sister shake off the stink of a summer sun from her shoulders.These red ants between my toes and slippers: how even when I think I am alone, I am not." are variations of original lines "I grip, as though for the first/ time, a paper bag/ of french fries from McDonald's,/ and lick, from each fingertip,/ the fat and salt as I stand alone" from the poem "En Route to Bangladesh, Another Crisis of Faith" by Tarfia Faizullah.

ACKNOWLEDGMENTS

Grateful acknowledgments are due to the editors of the following publications where many of these poems first appeared, or are forthcoming, albeit in slightly different forms, and often with changed titles:

Arsenic Lobster, Bitter Oleander, Bluestem, Bone Bouquet, Breakwater Review, burntdistrict, Cream City Review, Drunken Boat, Fjords Review, Infoxicated Corner, Juked, Los Angeles Review, lingerpost, Little Patuxent Review, Natural Bridge, New Delta Review, New South, Permafrost, PRISM International, Rappahannock Review, Rhino, South Dakota Review, Superstition Review, Tahoma Literary Review, The Four Quarters Magazine, This Magazine, Tusculum Review, West Branch.

Several of these poems also appeared in my chapbook *Lullabies Are Barbed Wire Nations*, published by Two of Cups Press.

These poems would not have happened without the teachers, mentors and friends at Poetry Barn (formerly Rooster Moans). Most of these poems began as tentative drafts in workshops at Poetry Barn, were vigorously critiqued by Susan Yount, Lissa Kiernan, Brenda Mann Hammack, Alexandra van Kamp, Maureen Alsop, Renee Emerson and Sara Tracey. I have often engaged with their poems in this book, arguing with their line-breaks, images and intonations while learning from them. I could not have asked for a better community to learn from. Sarah Rose Nordegren read many of these poems in their more nascent stage and offered extremely valuable critiques. The book is better for her incisive comments. Thank you!

Gabrielle Calvocoressi and Elizabeth Colen, for your encouragement and piercing questions. Many many thanks.

I could not have done this without the inspiration and love offered by Jenn Givhan and Alicia Elkort. Jenn has read many of these drafts repeatedly, offering patient comments. Alicia saw this "novel" even before I dared to dream about it. Thank you!

Leigh Anne Hornfeldt saw possibilities in Toi and Tombur in their not-yet-completed form. But, her acknowledgement gave me the courage to continue to imagine the life of my crazy twins. Without Fox Frazier-Foley and Jasmine An, though, they would not have ever existed in their present forms. To you two and the Agape Editions team, I owe my biggest gratitude.

To Vandana Khanna, thanks. Your affirmation meant *so much*!

To Mihir and Arjun, for providing the gossip, laughter and encouragement when I needed it most. To Dena, for teaching me how literary communities can be formed in many different ways. To Anubha, Manjiri and Usha, for all the support and love.

To Dennis, Pupai, and Pramod, for loving me in the way only they can.

To the inhabitants and the visitors of that three room house at Garia Station Road—the only place in this world I still call *home*—thanking you would seem like a *yankee nyakami*. Yet this book would not have existed without the stories created and sheltered there. In the same way, I would probably never have felt the need to write without the first lessons of creativity at our very own Ashani Natyam. To all the uncles and aunts there, who I always called by their first names, I would not dare trivialize the things you taught me by uttering a dry *thanks*. It is astounding how many people conspired to make an *antel* out of the little girl I once was.

The last poem in this book was written right after the HokKolorob movement stormed the Jadavpur University campus and the streets of Kolkata. As I observed the going-ons from afar, it became impossible to put my faith only in despair. Thus, this book would be impossible without the conversations I have had with Ratul, Munmun, Priyasmita, Amitabha, Kaushik, Bandana, Shubho, Titir, Agni, the Chitrangada contingent—Srirupa, Sriparna, Gargi, Trishnika, Aditya, and Juni. And many many others, too numerous to name.

This book is dedicated to all kolorobis anywhere in the world—those of the past, the present, the imagined and as-yet-unimagined futures. May we continue to create sounds that both break and make. But, more than anything else, this book is dedicated to the memory of Saral Bhattacharya, the youngest martyr our neighborhood could mourn and boast of.

www.ingramcontent.com/pod-product-compliance
Lightning Source LLC
Chambersburg PA
CBHW071739080526
44588CB00013B/2095